KB
The Business Coach

Disclaimer: The information contained herein is general in nature and for informative purposes only. It is based on the author's personal experience. The author assumes no responsibility whatsoever, under any circumstances, for any actions taken as a result of the information contained herein.

Copyright © 2020. Elite Markets Online LLC, & KB The Business Coach. All Rights Reserved. No part of this document may be reproduced or shared without express, written consent from the author

THANK YOU....

I want to start by saying thank you for investing in yourself and working with KB The Business Coach to begin and start your exciting journey to becoming an entrepreneur and starting a successful business.

This book is setup as an interactive printable guide so you can jot your ideas down and also print out the pages so you can see your ideas in motion.

If you have any questions or concerns while you are going through the book please feel free to email me at info@elitemarketsonline.com.

> **"EVERYONE HAS A KEY ITS JUST A MATTER OF USING IT!"**

GOOD LUCK AND I WISH YOU MUCH SUCCESS!!!

KB
The Business Coach

HELLO MY FELLOW ENTREPRENEURS!
WHO IS KB THE BUSINESS COACH?

- MBA Graduate
- Mother of 3
- Six Sigma Yellow Belt &
- Green Belt Training
- Former High School Business Teacher of 10 years
- Graphic Designer
- Goal Oriented
- Determined to help future entrepreneurs develop their own business, and create generational wealth.

I do want you to understand that this will be a hard process but not impossible. It will take consistency on your part and tenacity. But remain focused because the reward will be phenomenal.

I will be here with you along the way and will show how to go further and further in your business.

KB The Business Coach

This guide will serve as the basis to you starting your business. I will provide videos, webinars, digital e-books to help continue your business.

From marketing to advertising, to social media marketing, websites and more. I will provide you with more resources to you along the way.

So lets get started... Get your pen, paper, highlighters and post-its, and turn your thinking cap on and lets get started on the path to success.

WELCOME TO THE KICKSTARTING YOUR BUSINESS DIGITAL GUIDE!

Hello my new Business Associate and Fellow Entrepreneur.

So it all begins with a plan, anytime you begin a project, or a develop a new strategy its important to devise a plan on how it will be successful.

Its hard to know what the end result will be without having a plan, so its very important that we plan out your journey and your plan to developing your new business.

A business plan is the blueprint of your business, it works like a roadmap of what your business is and how it plans to grow and be successful.

The business plan will show you and anyone who is interested in your business what your business is all about!

Once again please understand that you have to be focused and consistent with this.

You will have late nights and early mornings, and coffee or some sort of caffeine will be your new BESTIE!

KB
The Business Coach

If you can answer yes to these questions then you are ready to start, if not please throw this book away!

- Are you willing to say no to friends and family when its time to get down to it and work on YOUR business?
- Are you able to survive on little sleep but still be able to function?
- Will you be consistent, even when you don't see the end?
- Are you ready to make sacrifices for your business?
- Are you able to wake up when you get that early morning bright idea and jot it down and plan it out?
- Do you want to successful and build a legacy for yourself or for your family?

If you answered yes to these questions, then lets get it started!

BECOME AN ENTREPRENEUR…WHY?

Why do you want to start a new business?

If you start a business who will it benefit and what does that mean to you?

KB
The Business Coach

LET'S THINK ABOUT THIS

Complete this sentence. When I think about me starting and running my own business, I envision....

WRITE IT ALL DOWN….

Use this arrow to write down your hobbies, your interests, your dreams your desires. What brings you the most joy and the most happiness. When I think about the easiest way to think about this, the one question that comes to my mind…. "What do you do effortlessly and without thinking?"

LET'S NARROW IT DOWN

Now that its all on paper, let's hone in on some of the ideas. Answer the questions below:

What do you just love to do in your free time?

If money was no object, what business would you start?

What's the first thing that comes to mind when you think of starting a business?

What could you get lost for hours doing?

What type of websites do you find yourself constantly visiting?

What stands out on these sites for you?

What is a common thread amongst them?

LET'S NARROW IT DOWN SOME MORE

What are some skills that come naturally to you?

What are some things you would love to invest more time into learning?

If you could go back to school or take a class on a subject what would it be?

List 3 skills you would love to get paid to do on a regular basis:

List 3-5 questions people are always asking you:

SO WHAT PROBLEM WILL YOU SOLVE?

The whole purpose of any business is to solve a problem. Think back at the skills and ideas and think now what will you solve.

For me, I enjoy teaching, I love business and showing others how to do things. Ive been told I could teach anything. Ive always had people call me and ask me to do stuff especially when it comes to business.

You have to take what you love to do into what people will pay you to do.

So lets look at my mode for my business:

Business Industry: Business & Entrepreneurship
Professional Business Idea: Teaching new business entrepreneurs how to start their own business.
Specific Audience: Everyday person who wants to be in business for themselves. Someone who has the drive and tenacity to be successful.

WHO IS YOUR IDEAL CLIENT?

Is your ideal client male or female?

Where do they live?

Are they employed or self-employed?

What do they do for a living?

WHO IS YOUR IDEAL CLIENT?

What is their income level?

How old are they?

Do they have children?

Are they tech savvy or technologically challenged?

YOUR IDEAL CLIENT

What brands or influencers are they following?

What are their goals and aspirations?

So the meat and potatoes....

What problems might they struggle with and how can you help them?

MOVING FORWARD...

So now we should have some idea on what direction that you want to go in and what your business model will be. And now its time for you to begin your business plan.

THE BUSINESS PLAN

What is a Business Plan?

A business plan is a formal statement of business goals, reasons they are attainable, and plans for reaching them. It may also contain background information about the organization or team attempting to reach those goals.

The Business Plan:
- Helps you run your business
- Guides you through each stage of starting and managing your business
- Acts as a roadmap of structure for your business
- Help you bring in new customers
- Allows you to eligible for funding

The are two categories/methods of a business plan:
- Traditional
- Lean Startup

We will complete your business plan using the traditional method.

COMPONENTS OF THE TRADITIONAL BUSINESS PLAN

1. Executive Summary
2. Company Description
3. Market Analysis
4. Organization & Management
5. Service/Product Line
6. Marketing & Sales
7. Funding Request
8. Financial Projections
9. New Businesses Financial Projections

1, THE EXECUTIVE SUMMARY

Tell your readers what your company is why it will be successful. Include your mission statement, your products or service and basic information about your leadership team, employees and location. Include financial information and a growth plans if you plan to ask for financing.

So what is your purpose, you are starting a business because why? What is your mission?
Lets answer some questions that will help you build your mission statement!!

What is the purpose of your brand?
_____
_____
_____
_____

When you think about being successful what comes to mind?
_____
_____
_____
_____

What do you owe your customers, what is your promise to them? _____
_____
_____
_____

There are 3 components to your mission statement.

1. **Key Market.** Who is your target audience?

_____
_____
_____
_____

2. **Contribution.** What is your product or service?

_____
_____
_____
_____

3. **Distinction.** What makes your product or service unique or why would the audience buy yours over the competitors?

_____
_____
_____

YOUR MISSION STATEMENT

Write your Mission Statement.

YOUR PRODUCTS/SERVICES

What type of physical products/services will you offer?

What will be the price?

2. COMPANY DESCRIPTION

The company description is the next section of the business plan it will provide a more detailed description about your business.

What issue does your business solve?

```
┌─────────────────────────────────────────────┐
│                                             │
│                                             │
│                                             │
│                                             │
└─────────────────────────────────────────────┘
```

Be specific, list your consumers and businesses that your company plans to serve.

```
┌─────────────────────────────────────────────┐
│                                             │
│                                             │
│                                             │
│                                             │
└─────────────────────────────────────────────┘
```

What is your competitive advantage that will make your business a success?

What are your strengths?

3. MARKET ANALYSIS

This is where you will include your findings about your market research.

What does the competitor do and how can you do it better and how?

Conduct research on your competition.

Check out their websites, their social media, what do they offer to their customers?

YOUR 1st COMPETITOR

Who is your competition?

What do they offer?

How are they similar to your business?

How are you different?

YOUR 2nd COMPETITOR

Who is your competition?

What do they offer?

How are they similar to your business?

How are you different?

YOUR 3rd COMPETITOR

Who is your competition?

What do they offer?

How are they similar to your business?

How are you different?

YOUR 4th COMPETITOR

Who is your competition?

What do they offer?

How are they similar to your business?

How are you different?

4. ORGANIZATION MANAGEMENT

Tell your reader how your company will be structured and who will run the business. What's your legal structure? Use an organizational structure and show what they bring to the business? Include resumes of your key members

The business structure that you choose will have an impact on your day to day operations, your taxes and how much of your personal assets that you are willing to use.

Lets look at the legal structures and lets figure out where your business lies.

TYPES OF BUSINESS STRUCTURES

Sole proprietorship

A sole proprietorship is easy to form and gives you complete control of your business. You're automatically considered to be a sole proprietorship if you do business activities but don't register as any other kind of business.

Sole proprietorships do not produce a separate business entity. This means your business assets and liabilities are not separate from your personal assets and liabilities. You can be held personally liable for the debts and obligations of the business. Sole proprietors are still able to get a trade name. It can also be hard to raise money because you can't sell stock, and banks are hesitant to lend to sole proprietorships.

Sole proprietorships can be a good choice for low-risk businesses and owners who want to test their business idea before forming a more formal business.

Partnership

Partnerships are the simplest structure for two or more people to own a business together. There are two common kinds of partnerships: limited partnerships (LP) and limited liability partnerships (LLP).

Limited partnerships have only one general partner with unlimited liability, and all other partners have limited liability. The partners with limited liability also tend to have limited control over the company, which is documented in a partnership agreement. Profits are passed through to personal tax returns, and the general partner — the partner without limited liability — must also pay self-employment taxes.

Limited liability partnerships are similar to limited partnerships, but give limited liability to every owner. An LLP protects each partner from debts against the partnership, they won't be responsible for the actions of other partners.

Partnerships can be a good choice for businesses with multiple owners, professional groups (like attorneys), and groups who want to test their business idea before forming a more formal business.

Limited liability company (LLC)

An LLC lets you take advantage of the benefits of both the corporation and partnership business structures.

LLCs protect you from personal liability in most instances, your personal assets — like your vehicle, house, and savings accounts — won't be at risk in case your LLC faces bankruptcy or lawsuits.

Profits and losses can get passed through to your personal income without facing corporate taxes. However, members of an LLC are considered self-employed and must pay self-employment tax contributions towards Medicare and Social Security.

LLCs can have a limited life in many states. When a member joins or leaves an LLC, some states may require the LLC to be dissolved and re-formed with new membership — unless there's already an agreement in place within the LLC for buying, selling, and transferring ownership.

LLCs can be a good choice for medium- or higher-risk businesses, owners with significant personal assets they want to be protected, and owners who want to pay a lower tax rate than they would with a corporation.

Corporation

C corp

A corporation, sometimes called a C corp, is a legal entity that's separate from its owners. Corporations can make a profit, be taxed, and can be held legally liable.

Corporations offer the strongest protection to its owners from personal liability, but the cost to form a corporation is higher than other structures. Corporations also require more extensive record-keeping, operational processes, and reporting.

Unlike sole proprietors, partnerships, and LLCs, corporations pay income tax on their profits. In some cases, corporate profits are taxed twice — first, when the company makes a profit, and again when dividends are paid to shareholders on their personal tax returns.

Corporations have a completely independent life separate from its shareholders. If a shareholder leaves the company or sells his or her shares, the C corp can continue doing business relatively undisturbed.

Corporations have an advantage when it comes to raising capital because they can raise funds through the sale of stock, which can also be a benefit in attracting employees.

Corporations can be a good choice for medium- or higher-risk businesses, businesses that need to raise money, and businesses that plan to "go public" or eventually be sold.

S corp

An S corporation, sometimes called an S corp, is a special type of corporation that's designed to avoid the double taxation drawback of regular C corps. S corps allow profits, and some losses, to be passed through directly to owners' personal income without ever being subject to corporate tax rates.

Not all states tax S corps equally, but most recognize them the same way the federal government does and taxes the shareholders accordingly. Some states tax S corps on profits above a specified limit and other states don't recognize the S corp election at all, simply treating the business as a C corp.

S corps must file with the IRS to get S corp status, a different process from [registering with their state](#).

There are special limits on S corps. S corps can't have more than 100 shareholders, and all shareholders must be U.S. citizens. You'll still have to follow strict filing and operational processes of a C corp.

S corps also have an independent life, just like C corps. If a shareholder leaves the company or sells his or her shares, the S corp can continue doing business relatively undisturbed.

S corps can be a good choice for a businesses that would otherwise be a C corp, but meet the criteria to file as an S corp.

B corp

A benefit corporation, sometimes called a B corp, is a for-profit corporation recognized by a majority of U.S. states. B corps are different from C corps in purpose, accountability, and transparency, but aren't different in how they're taxed.

B corps are driven by both mission and profit. Shareholders hold the company accountable to produce some sort of public benefit in addition to a financial profit. Some states require B corps to submit annual benefit reports that demonstrate their contribution to the public good.

There are several third-party B corp certification services, but none are required for a company to be legally considered a B corp in a state where the legal status is available.

Close corporation

Close corporations resemble B corps but have a less traditional corporate structure. These shed many formalities that typically govern corporations and apply to smaller companies.

State rules vary, but shares are usually barred from public trading. Close corporations can be run by a small group of shareholders without a board of directors.

Nonprofit corporation

Nonprofit corporations are organized to do charity, education, religious, literary, or scientific work. Because their work benefits the public, nonprofits can receive tax-exempt status, meaning they don't pay state or federal taxes income taxes on any profits it makes.

Nonprofits must file with the IRS to get tax exemption, a different process from [registering with their state](#).

Nonprofit corporations need to follow organizational rules very similar to a regular C corp. They also need to follow special rules about what they do with any profits they earn. For example, they can't distribute profits to members or political campaigns.

Nonprofits are often called 501(c)(3) corporations — a reference to the section of the Internal Revenue Code that is most commonly used to grant tax-exempt status.

Cooperative

A cooperative is a business or organization owned by and operated for the benefit of those using its services. Profits and earnings generated by the cooperative are distributed among the members, also known as user-owners. Typically, an elected board of directors and officers run the cooperative while regular members have voting power to control the direction of the cooperative. Members can become part of the cooperative by purchasing shares, though the amount of shares they hold does not affect the weight of their vote.

Business Structures

The above information may have been a lot, but it breaks down the different types of structures but it gives you a complete breakdown of all of the structures so that you can choose the correct one.

View the chart below for a basic breakdown:

Business structure	Ownership	Liability	Taxes
Sole proprietorship	One person	Unlimited personal liability	Personal tax only
Partnerships	Two or more people	Unlimited personal liability unless structured as a limited partnership	Self-employment tax (except for limited partners) Personal tax
Limited liability company (LLC)	One or more people	Owners are not personally liable	Self-employment tax Personal tax or corporate tax
Corporation - C corp	One or more people	Owners are not personally liable	Corporate tax
Corporation - S corp	One or more people, but no more than 100, and all must be U.S. citizens	Owners are not personally liable	Personal tax
Corporation - B corp	One or more people	Owners are not personally liable	Corporate tax
Corporation - Nonprofit	One or more people	Owners are not personally liable	Tax-exempt, but corporate profits can't be distributed

In this section you can also include resumes of your workers. This will provide back up information of each worker and it allow you to have this information on hard.

INSERT RESUMES HERE

5. SERVICES / PRODUCT LINE

Describe what you sell or what services you offer Explain the benefits of your products,

What products/services do you sell?

PRODUCT LIFE CYCLE

The product life cycle is the process a product goes through from when it is first introduced into the market until it declines or is removed from the market.

What is your product life cycle?

Intellectual Property

Intellectual property is a category of property that includes intangible creations of the human intellect. There are many types of intellectual property, and some countries recognize more than others. The most well-known types are copyrights, patents, trademarks, and trade secrets.

Future Products & Upcoming Research

If you have some things that you want to put to paper but will work on later you can add it hear.

Do you have any future products that you will be working on?

Is there any upcoming research you will be working on?

6. **MARKETING & SALES**

How will you attract and retain your customers?

How does a sale actually take place?

What does your day look like?

What do you plan to do on a day to day basis for your business?
 Emails? Content Creation? Marketing? Social Media? Client Work or Consults? Promotions?

Your Business Process

Write Out What Would Be Your Ideal Productive Day From Start to Finish. How many hours do you want to work each day? How will you structure your day?

YOUR

ARE

ALMOST

FINISH

WITH

YOUR

BUSINESS

PLAN

DON'T FORGET, CONSISTENCY AND TENACITY

7. Funding Request

Outline your funding requirements Debt or Equity, Terms and length of time Detailed description of how you will use the funds Description of how you will pay your debt. If you plan on getting a loan you will use this area to write in the above information. Some small business or startups don't require startup money, but some do and will require some financing.

8. FINANCIAL PROJECTIONS

Supplement your funding request with financial projections Convince the reader that your business is stable. So if you do need funding for your business you have to convince the ready that your business is stable and able to profit. Sell yourself.

9. NEW BUSINESSES FINANCIAL PROJECTIONS

Include prospective financial outlook for the 1st year Be specific and use quarterly or even monthly projections about your business Be clear and use charts This information should match your funding request.

ESTABLISHED BUSINESS FINANCIAL PROJECTIONS

If you consider yourself an established business who have been in business for 3-5 years you will need to include the following.

Include income statements and balance sheets and cash flow statements for the last 3 - 5 years If you have collateral you could put against the loan, list it here Provide an outlook for the next five year

APPENDIX

The last section of the Business Plan is the Appendix. In the appendix include the following components:

- RESUMES
- PRODUCT PICTURES
- LETTERS OF REFERENCES
- LICENSES & PERMITS
- PATENTS
- LEGAL DOCUMENTS
- PERMITS
- CONTRACTS

Congratulations you have completed your business plan. WooHoo, that wasn't so bad was it. The good thing about it, its DONE!!!!!

We are gonna look at a few more components that will give you the next steps after the business plan so you can get your business moving.

What Next? These are just some things to consider when starting your business and can serve as the next step for you if you haven't started already.

So What Do You Need To Operate Your Business?

Website:

Domain:

Hosting:

Logo Design:

Graphics:

Hosting:

Coaching/Consults:

Product Creation:

Inventory Investment:

And we are almost at the finish line. You should feel accomplished you have put in a lot of work and a lot of hours into this guide.

I want you to consider some very important things that I wish someone would have told me about and that's time management.

You cant do it all, and some things may need to be delegated so you can fully function your business. Now in the beginning as you build your clientele you will be able to do everything by yourself but as clientele grows you will need to develop systems so that you can work on your business, products and services.

The Sharing of Tasks

This section will come with time and as your business begins to grow you will need to think about.

What are some tasks that you will begin doing in your business that could possibly be delegated to someone.

What are some tasks that can be delegated to someone else?

And You are Done !

Congrats you made it and you have successfully developed your business plan and you are ready to create generational wealth.

I would enjoy learning about what your business is and how the process is coming. I will be available for questions or even a private consultation.

You can visit me online at the following locations:

WWW.ELITEMARKETSONLINE.COM

WWW.KBTHEBUSINESSCOACH.COM

Facebook: KB The Business Coach

Instagram: KB The Business Coach

Phone: 502.354.8301

Email: info@elitemarketsonline.com

Thanks,

KB The Business Coach

KB The Business Coach

www.ingramcontent.com/pod-product-compliance
Lightning Source LLC
Chambersburg PA
CBHW080952220526
45465CB00008BA/3255